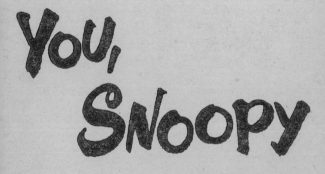

YOU, SNOOPY

Selected cartoons from
SNOOPY COME HOME :

By Charles M. Schulz

A FAWCETT CREST BOOK
Fawcett Publications, Inc., Greenwich, Conn.

WE LOVE YOU, SNOOPY

This book, prepared especially for Fawcett Publications, Inc., was selected from SNOOPY COME HOME, and is reprinted by arrangement with Holt, Rinehart and Winston, Inc.

Published by Fawcett World Library
67 West 44th Street, New York, N.Y. 10036
Printed in the United States of America